~A BINGO BOOK~

# Maine
# Bingo Book

## COMPLETE BINGO GAME IN A BOOK

Written By Rebecca Stark
**Educational Books 'n' Bingo**

ISBN 978-0-87386-512-8

**Educational Books 'n' Bingo**

Printed in the U.S.A.

# DIRECTIONS

**INCLUDED:**

List of Terms

Templates for Additional Terms and Clues

2 Clues per Term

30 Unique Bingo Cards

Markers

1.  **Either cut apart the book or make copies of ALL the sheets. You might want to make an extra copy of the clue sheets to use for introduction and review. Keep the sheets in an envelope for easy reuse.**

2.  Cut apart the call cards with terms and clues.

3.  Pass out one bingo card per student. There are enough for a class of 30.

4.  Pass out markers. You may cut apart the markers included in this book or use any other small items of your choice.

5.  Decide whether or not you will require the entire card to be filled. Requiring the entire card to be filled provides a better review. However, if you have a short time to fill, you may prefer to have them do the just the border or some other format. Tell the class before you begin what is required.

6.  There are 50 terms. Read the list before you begin. If there are any terms that have not been covered in class, you may want to read to the students the term and clues before you begin.

7.  There is a blank space in the middle of each card. You can instruct the students to use it as a free space or you can write in answers to cover terms not included. Of course, in this case you would create your own clues. (Templates provided.)

8.  Shuffle the cards and place them in a pile. Two or three clues are provided for each term. If you plan to play the game with the same group more than once, you might want to choose a different clue for each game. If not, you may choose to use more than one clue.

9.  Be sure to keep the cards you have used for the present game in a separate pile. When a student calls, "Bingo," he or she will have to verify that the correct answers are on his or her card AND that the markers were placed in response to the proper questions. Pull out the cards that are on the student's card keeping them in the order they were used in the game. Read each clue as it was given and ask the student to identify the correct answer from his or her card.

10. If the student has the correct answers on the card AND has shown that they were marked in response to the *correct questions,* then that student is the winner and the game is over. If the student does not have the correct answers on the card OR he or she marked the answers in response to *the wrong questions,* then the game continues until there is a proper winner.

11. If you want to play again, reshuffle the cards and begin again.

## Have fun!

# TERMS INCLUDED

| | |
|---|---|
| Acadia | Judicial Branch |
| American Revolution | King Philip |
| Aroostook Plateau | William King |
| Atlantic Ocean | Landlocked Salmon |
| Augusta | Legislative Branch |
| Bangor | Lewiston |
| Bar Harbor | Lobster(s) |
| Blueberry (-ies) | Henry Wadsworth Longfellow |
| Border(s) | Massachusetts Bay |
| Canada | Missouri Compromise |
| Castine | Moose |
| Coastal Lowlands | Moosehead |
| Coat of Arms | Motto |
| Coon Cat | New England |
| Counties | Nicknames |
| Crop | Penobscot |
| Dominion of New England | Portland |
| Down East | River(s) |
| Eastern New England Uplands | State |
| Executive Branch | Timber |
| Flag | Treaty of Paris |
| French Canadians | Wabanaki Confederacy |
| Estêvão Gomes | Webster-Ashburton Treaty |
| Sir Ferdinando Gorges | White Pine |
| Industries | White Mountains |

# Additional Terms

Choose as many additional terms as you would like and write them in the squares. Repeat each as desired.
Cut out the squares and randomly distribute them to the class.
Instruct the students to place their square on the center space of their card.

| | | | | |
|---|---|---|---|---|
| | | | | |
| | | | | |
| | | | | |
| | | | | |
| | | | | |
| | | | | |

Maine Bingo

# Clues for Additional Terms

Write three clues for each of your additional terms.

| | |
|---|---|
| _____<br>1.<br><br>2.<br><br>3. | _____<br>1.<br><br>2.<br><br>3. |
| _____<br>1.<br><br>2.<br><br>3. | _____<br>1.<br><br>2.<br><br>3. |
| _____<br>1.<br><br>2.<br><br>3. | _____<br>1.<br><br>2.<br><br>3. |

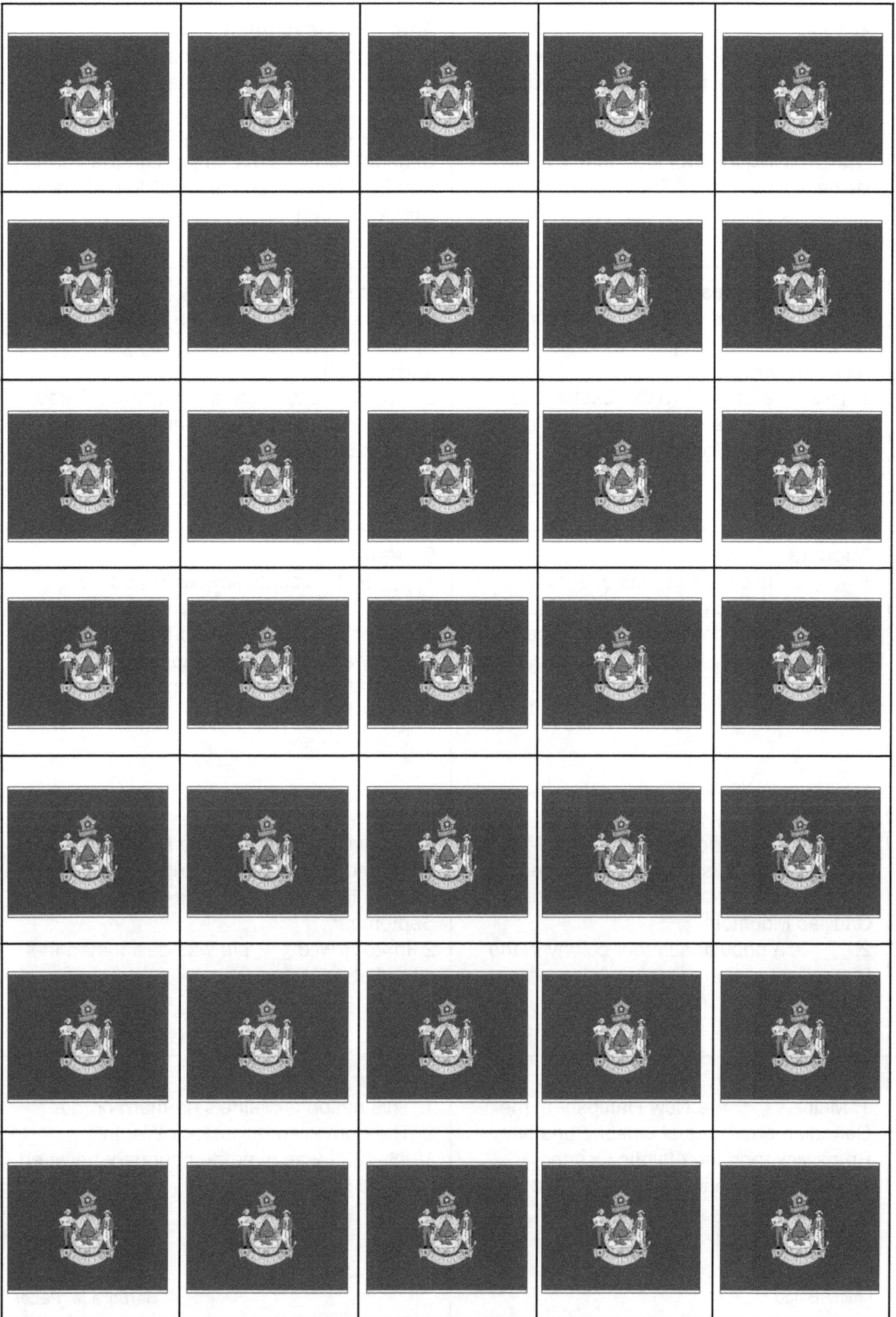

| | |
|---|---|
| **Acadia**<br>1. ____ National Park is on Mt. Desert Island. It was the first national park east of the Mississippi.<br>2. ____ was the name of a colony of New France. It included an area that is now Maine. | **American Revolution**<br>1. The unsuccessful Penobscot Expedition was the largest American naval expedition of the ____.<br>2. Many Maine men were part of Col. Benedict Arnold's march through the north woods of Maine in his attempt to capture Quebec during the ____. |
| **Aroostook Plateau**<br>1. The ____ is in the northeast section of the Eastern New England Uplands. It is a very fertile region.<br>2. This area of Eastern the Eastern New England Uplands has the best farmland. Most of the potato farms are here. | **Atlantic Ocean**<br>1. Maine is bordered on the east and south by the ____. The coastline is jagged and mostly rocky.<br>2. Maine's history and economy are linked to vast its timber reserves and to the sea— in this case, the ____. |
| **Augusta**<br>1. ____ is the capital of Maine.<br>2. It is the third-smallest state capital after Montpelier, Vermont, and Pierre, South Dakota. | **Bangor**<br>1. ____ is the county seat of Penobscot County. It is a major commercial and cultural center of eastern and northern Maine.<br>2. ____ was the Lumber Capital of the World in the 1800s. The first sawmill was built there in 1772. |
| **Bar Harbor**<br>1. ____ is on the northeast shore of Mount Desert Island. It is home to the largest parts of Acadia National Park, including Cadillac Mountain.<br>2. ____ is a popular summer colony in the Down East region of Maine. It is also a popular stop for cruise ships. | **Blueberry (-ies)**<br>1. The wild ____ is the state fruit. Wild ____ are found mostly on hilly and rocky terrain and are in season from late July to early September.<br>2. In 2011 wild ____ pie was designated the official state dessert. |
| **Border(s)**<br>1. Maine's ____ are New Hampshire, the Canadian provinces of Quebec and New Brunswick, and the Atlantic Ocean.<br>2. Maine is the only state to ____ just one other state. | **Canada**<br>1. This nation is Maine's northern border.<br>2. The nonviolent Aroostook War in 1838–1839 was over the boundary between ____ and Maine. |

| Castine | Coastal Lowlands |
|---|---|
| 1. One of the oldest towns in New England, ___ is situated on Penobscot Bay near the site of Fort Pentagouet. The Maine Maritime Academy is in ___.<br>2. ___ served as the capital of Acadia from 1670–1674. | 1. The ___ start at the Atlantic Ocean and extend from ten to forty miles inland.<br>2. The ___ area is characterized by flat, sandy beaches in the south and small, sandy beaches in small inlets between the higher cliffs in the north. West of the beaches are salt marshes and tidal creeks. |
| **Coat of Arms**<br>1. The state ___ depicts a shield. A pine tree, a moose, land, and sea are on the shield.<br>2. On either side of the shield on the state ___ are a seaman resting on an anchor and a farmer resting on a scythe. Above the shield is the state motto. | **Coon Cat**<br>1. The Maine ___ is the official state cat.<br>2. The Maine ___ has a thick, glossy, water-resistant coat that is well suited for New England winters. |
| **Counties**<br>1. There are 16 ___ in Maine.<br>2. The most populous ___ tend to be located in the southwest along the Atlantic seaboard. The largest in terms of land area are inland. | **Crop**<br>1. Blueberries are an important ___. Maine's blueberry harvest is the largest in the nation.<br>2. Potatoes are another important ___. They are grown in the Aroostook Plateau. |
| **Dominion of New England**<br>1. In 1686 King James II created the ___, which comprised Massachusetts, Vermont, New Hampshire, Connecticut, and Rhode Island and later New York, and East and West Jersey.<br>2. This administrative union of English colonies failed because it was too large for one governor to manage. | **Down East**<br>1. The name stems from the fact when ships sailed from Boston to Maine, the wind was at their backs, so they were sailing downwind.<br>2. ___ refers to the coast of Maine from Penobscot Bay to the Canadian border. It is sometimes used as a loose term for the entire eastern portion of the state. |
| **Eastern New England Uplands**<br>1. The ___ are between the Coastal Lowlands and the White Mountains. This region is about twenty to fifty miles wide and rises from sea level to about 2,000 feet.<br>2. The Aroostook Plateau is in the northern part of the ___. The Longfellow Mountains run through the center of the region. | **Executive Branch**<br>1. The ___ is responsible for execution of the laws created by the legislature; it comprises the governor and several departments.<br>2. The governor is head of the ___. The present-day governor is [fill in]. |

| | |
|---|---|
| **Flag**<br>1. The state ___ displays Maine's coat-of-arms.<br>2. The state ___ has a blue field. It is the same shade of blue as on the ___ of the United States. | **French Canadians**<br>1. In the late 19th century, many ___ arrived from Quebec and New Brunswick to work in the textile-mill cities.<br>2. Many ___ settled in Aroostook and Androscoggin counties as well as in the Lewiston-Auburn area. |
| **Estêvão Gomes**<br>1. ___ was a Portuguese cartographer and explorer.<br>2. In 1524 ___ explored present-day Nova Scotia, sailing south along the Maine coast. | **Sir Ferdinando Gorges**<br>1. In 1622 ___ and John Mason received a land patent for the Province of Maine.<br>2. In 1629 ___ and John Mason divided the Province of Maine, with Mason's portion becoming the Province of New Hampshire. |
| **Industries**<br>1. At one time the most important ___ in Maine were shipbuilding and lumber.<br>2. Today the most important ___ are papermaking and the manufacture of wood products. Maine has the largest paper-production capacity in the nation. | **Judicial Branch**<br>1. The ___ is responsible for interpreting the laws.<br>2. The ___ comprises several courts, the highest of which is the Supreme Court. |
| **King Philip**<br>1. ___'s real name was Metacomet. He was the chief of the Wampanoag Indians.<br>2. ___'s War was a conflict between Native Americans and English colonists and their Native American allies in 1675–78. | **William King**<br>1. ___ became the first governor of Maine when it separated from Massachusetts in 1820.<br>2. ___, a merchant and shipbuilder, was the first governor of the state of Maine. |
| **Landlocked Salmon**<br>1. The ___ is the state fish.<br>2. The ___, a subspecies of the Atlantic salmon, never reaches the sea. The Sebago salmon, commonly found in Maine, is an example. | **Legislative Branch**<br>1. The ___ is responsible for making the laws.<br>2. The ___ comprises the Senate and the House of Representatives. The Senate has 35 members and the House has 151 members; they are elected every two years. |

Maine Bingo

| | |
|---|---|
| **Lewiston**<br>1. This city in Androscoggin County is the second-largest city in the state.<br>2. A former industrial center, ___ is in south-central Maine, at the falls of the Androscoggin River. | **Lobster(s)**<br>1. Maine is famous for its shellfish, especially clams and ___.<br>2. Maine's yearly ___ catch is larger than that of any other state. |
| **Henry Wadsworth Longfellow**<br>1. This famous poet was born on February 27, 1807, in Portland, Maine. It was part of Massachusetts at the time.<br>2. His best known works include "Paul Revere's Ride," "The Song of Hiawatha," and "Evangeline." | **Massachusetts Bay**<br>1. The Province of Maine was absorbed into the ___ Colony in the 1650s.<br>2. The territory administered by the ___ Colony included much of present-day central New England. |
| **Missouri Compromise**<br>1. Maine seceded from the Commonwealth of Massachusetts and became the 23rd state on March 15, 1820. This was done as part of the ___.<br>2. The ___ provided that Missouri would be admitted into the Union as a slave state and Maine as a free state. | **Moose**<br>1. The ___ is the official state animal.<br>2. The ___ is the largest member of the deer family. A bull may stand more than 6 feet high at the shoulder and weigh more than 1,400 lbs. |
| **Moosehead**<br>1. ___ is the largest lake in Maine and the largest mountain lake in the eastern United States.<br>2. Sebago is the deepest lake in Maine. It is also the second largest lake in the state. Only ___ is larger. | **Motto**<br>1. The state ___ is *"Dirigo,"* which translates to "I lead."<br>2. The state ___, *"Dirigo,"* is on the state coat of arms, which is on both the state flag and the state seal. |
| **New England**<br>1. Maine is both the northernmost and the easternmost portion of ___.<br>2. ___ comprises six states: Maine, New Hampshire, Vermont, Massachusetts, Rhode Island, and Connecticut. | **Nicknames**<br>1. The Pine Tree State is the most common of several ___ for Maine.<br>2. The following are all ___ for Maine: Pine Tree State, Lumber State, Border State, Old Dirigo State, Switzerland of America, and Polar Star State. |

Maine Bingo

| **Penobscot**<br>1. The ___ are part of the Wabanaki Confederacy along with the Abenaki, Passamaquoddy, Maliseet, and Mi'kmaq nations.<br>2. The ___ Indian Island Reservation is near Old Town, Maine. Madockawando was a sachem of the ___ Indians. | **Portland**<br>1. ___ is the largest city in Maine.<br>2. Fort Levett in the harbor is named for naval captain Christopher Levett, the first European settler of ___. |
|---|---|
| **River(s)**<br>1. The Androscoggin, Kennebec, Penobscot, and St. John are important ___ of Maine.<br>2. The Penobscot ___ is best known for its large historic salmon run. | **State**<br>1. Before Maine became a ___, it was part of the Commonwealth of Massachusetts and was called the District of Maine.<br>2. Maine seceded from Massachusetts and became the 23rd ___ on March 15, 1820. |
| **Timber**<br>1. ___ is an important natural resource in the state, and in colonial days shipbuilding was important.<br>2. ___ is an important resource. The forests provide the raw resources for manufactured products such as cardboard boxes, paper bags, wood pulp, and paper. | **Treaty of Paris**<br>1. The ___ ended the French and Indian War. 2. As part of the ___ of 1763, France ceded Canada and its dependencies to Great Britain. This included what is present-day Maine. |
| **Wabanaki Confederacy**<br>1. The ___ was a coalition of five Algonquian tribes of the eastern seaboard; they banded together in response to Iroquois aggression.<br>2. The ___ included the Abenaki, the Penobscot, the Maliseet, the Passamaquoddy, and the Mi'kmaq. | **Webster-Ashburton Treaty**<br>1. The ___ of 1842 established the Maine's northeast boundary, giving most of the disputed area to Maine.<br>2. The ___, was negotiated in 1842 by U.S. Secretary of State Daniel Webster and English special minister Lord Ashburton. |
| **White Mountains**<br>1. The ___ region is the westernmost of Maine's three geographic regions. The ___ cover a small portion of western Maine.<br>2. Mount Katahdin, Maine's highest point, is found in this region. | **White Pine**<br>1. ___ is the state tree. It is considered to be the largest conifer in the northeastern United States.<br>2. The ___ cone and tassel was adopted as the official floral emblem of Maine in 1895. |

Maine Bingo

# Maine Bingo

| Moosehead | Acadia | Aroostook Plateau | Eastern New England Uplands | Augusta |
|---|---|---|---|---|
| Dominion of New England | American Revolution | Wabanaki Confederacy | William King | Nicknames |
| Treaty of Paris | King Philip | | Massachusetts Bay | Webster-Ashburton Treaty |
| Timber | New England | State | Landlocked Salmon | Lewiston |
| Henry Wadsworth Longfellow | French Canadians | Coon Cat | Portland | White Pine |

Maine Bingo: Card No. 1

# Maine Bingo

| Timber | Treaty of Paris | Sir Ferdinando Gorges | Motto | Judicial Branch |
|---|---|---|---|---|
| Lewiston | Counties | Blueberry (-ies) | New England | Lobster(s) |
| Canada | French Canadians | | Estêvão Gomes | State |
| Missouri Compromise | Moose | King Philip | White Mountains | Augusta |
| Nicknames | Wabanaki Confederacy | Coon Cat | Dominion of New England | Portland |

Maine Bingo: Card No. 2

# Maine Bingo

| French Canadians | State | Counties | Landlocked Salmon | Treaty of Paris |
|---|---|---|---|---|
| Lewiston | American Revolution | Border(s) | Acadia | Flag |
| New England | Wabanaki Confederacy | | Lobster(s) | Atlantic Ocean |
| King Philip | Canada | Henry Wadsworth Longfellow | Missouri Compromise | Sir Ferdinando Gorges |
| Portland | Castine | Coon Cat | White Mountains | Judicial Branch |

Maine Bingo: Card No. 3

# Maine Bingo

| King Philip | Lobster(s) | Aroostook Plateau | Castine | Judicial Branch |
|---|---|---|---|---|
| Legislative Branch | Bar Harbor | Acadia | Motto | Treaty of Paris |
| Massachusetts Bay | Missouri Compromise | | White Pine | Eastern New England Uplands |
| State | American Revolution | Wabanaki Confederacy | Coon Cat | Blueberry (-ies) |
| Coastal Lowlands | Nicknames | Bangor | Portland | Webster-Ashburton Treaty |

# Maine Bingo

| Nicknames | Augusta | New England | Blueberry (-ies) | Castine |
|---|---|---|---|---|
| Legislative Branch | State | Border(s) | Estêvão Gomes | American Revolution |
| Aroostook Plateau | Webster-Ashburton Treaty | | William King | Executive Branch |
| White Pine | Judicial Branch | Moosehead | White Mountains | Coat of Arms |
| Counties | Coon Cat | Treaty of Paris | King Philip | Massachusetts Bay |

# Maine Bingo

| Atlantic Ocean | Lobster(s) | Sir Ferdinando Gorges | Judicial Branch | Webster-Ashburton Treaty |
|---|---|---|---|---|
| Landlocked Salmon | New England | Coat of Arms | Acadia | Treaty of Paris |
| Motto | Coastal Lowlands | | Bar Harbor | Estêvão Gomes |
| Coon Cat | Henry Wadsworth Longfellow | White Mountains | Bangor | Aroostook Plateau |
| Lewiston | Blueberry (-ies) | Moosehead | Massachusetts Bay | Crop |

Maine Bingo: Card No. 6

# Maine Bingo

| Moosehead | Lobster(s) | Executive Branch | State | Counties |
|---|---|---|---|---|
| Lewiston | Judicial Branch | French Canadians | American Revolution | Legislative Branch |
| Webster-Ashburton Treaty | Eastern New England Uplands | | Estêvão Gomes | Bar Harbor |
| King Philip | Missouri Compromise | Border(s) | Timber | Canada |
| Coon Cat | Castine | White Mountains | Bangor | Atlantic Ocean |

# Maine Bingo

| Massachusetts Bay | Lobster(s) | Down East | Landlocked Salmon | Bar Harbor |
|---|---|---|---|---|
| Legislative Branch | Aroostook Plateau | Motto | Webster-Ashburton Treaty | Blueberry (-ies) |
| Crop | Castine | | Judicial Branch | Augusta |
| Portland | King Philip | Timber | Coastal Lowlands | Missouri Compromise |
| Wabanaki Confederacy | Coon Cat | Bangor | New England | Lewiston |

# Maine Bingo

| Estêvão Gomes | Counties | French Canadians | Crop | Castine |
|---|---|---|---|---|
| Coastal Lowlands | Judicial Branch | Massachusetts Bay | New England | Lobster(s) |
| Flag | Moosehead | | American Revolution | Down East |
| Coat of Arms | Augusta | Henry Wadsworth Longfellow | William King | Executive Branch |
| Missouri Compromise | White Mountains | Border(s) | Timber | White Pine |

Maine Bingo: Card No. 9

# Maine Bingo

| Timber | Landlocked Salmon | Bar Harbor | Motto | Crop |
|---|---|---|---|---|
| Webster-Ashburton Treaty | Blueberry (-ies) | Acadia | American Revolution | Judicial Branch |
| Castine | Lobster(s) | | Eastern New England Uplands | Canada |
| Henry Wadsworth Longfellow | White Pine | Coat of Arms | White Mountains | Flag |
| Border(s) | Lewiston | Sir Ferdinando Gorges | Nicknames | Massachusetts Bay |

# Maine Bingo

| | | | | |
|---|---|---|---|---|
| Atlantic Ocean | Lobster(s) | New England | Coat of Arms | Lewiston |
| Down East | Flag | William King | Estêvão Gomes | Acadia |
| Legislative Branch | Judicial Branch | | Sir Ferdinando Gorges | French Canadians |
| Border(s) | Treaty of Paris | White Mountains | Castine | Timber |
| Coastal Lowlands | Coon Cat | Moosehead | Bangor | Counties |

# Maine Bingo

| Counties | Augusta | Flag | Landlocked Salmon | Estêvão Gomes |
|---|---|---|---|---|
| French Canadians | Lewiston | Aroostook Plateau | Bangor | American Revolution |
| Moosehead | Executive Branch | | Webster-Ashburton Treaty | Motto |
| Coon Cat | Missouri Compromise | Judicial Branch | Timber | Legislative Branch |
| Lobster(s) | Down East | Castine | Coastal Lowlands | Blueberry (-ies) |

Maine Bingo: Card No. 12

# Maine Bingo

| Coat of Arms | Augusta | Atlantic Ocean | Flag | Webster-Ashburton Treaty |
|---|---|---|---|---|
| Aroostook Plateau | Down East | Judicial Branch | Estêvão Gomes | Canada |
| Landlocked Salmon | Blueberry (-ies) | | French Canadians | Executive Branch |
| Massachusetts Bay | White Mountains | Bar Harbor | Castine | Timber |
| Coon Cat | White Pine | Bangor | Moosehead | William King |

# Maine Bingo

| Dominion of New England | Judicial Branch | New England | Estêvão Gomes | Coastal Lowlands |
|---|---|---|---|---|
| Blueberry (-ies) | Moosehead | Flag | American Revolution | Lobster(s) |
| Coat of Arms | Eastern New England Uplands | | Sir Ferdinando Gorges | Border(s) |
| White Pine | White Mountains | Castine | Bar Harbor | Atlantic Ocean |
| Coon Cat | Motto | Canada | Lewiston | Massachusetts Bay |

# Maine Bingo

| William King | Estêvão Gomes | New England | Counties | Landlocked Salmon |
|---|---|---|---|---|
| Atlantic Ocean | Sir Ferdinando Gorges | Acadia | Aroostook Plateau | Coastal Lowlands |
| Webster-Ashburton Treaty | Moosehead | | Treaty of Paris | Lobster(s) |
| Coon Cat | Flag | Down East | White Mountains | Coat of Arms |
| Lewiston | Missouri Compromise | Bangor | Crop | French Canadians |

# Maine Bingo

| Bar Harbor | Flag | Down East | Crop | Moose |
|---|---|---|---|---|
| Motto | Canada | Executive Branch | Legislative Branch | Eastern New England Uplands |
| Coat of Arms | Augusta | | Webster-Ashburton Treaty | French Canadians |
| King Philip | Blueberry (-ies) | Coon Cat | William King | Timber |
| Coastal Lowlands | River(s) | Bangor | Missouri Compromise | Lobster(s) |

Maine Bingo: Card No. 16

# Maine Bingo

| Border(s) | Penobscot | Industries | Flag | Dominion of New England |
|---|---|---|---|---|
| William King | Coastal Lowlands | White Mountains | Eastern New England Uplands | Executive Branch |
| Estêvão Gomes | Massachusetts Bay | | River(s) | Down East |
| White Pine | Lewiston | Timber | New England | Canada |
| Henry Wadsworth Longfellow | Coat of Arms | Counties | Landlocked Salmon | Augusta |

# Maine Bingo

| | | | | |
|---|---|---|---|---|
| Crop | Castine | Blueberry (-ies) | Coat of Arms | Motto |
| Lobster(s) | Border(s) | Henry Wadsworth Longfellow | Webster-Ashburton Treaty | Coastal Lowlands |
| Estêvão Gomes | Canada | | Industries | Aroostook Plateau |
| Augusta | Acadia | White Mountains | Timber | Sir Ferdinando Gorges |
| River(s) | Flag | New England | Penobscot | Atlantic Ocean |

# Maine Bingo

| | | | | |
|---|---|---|---|---|
| Webster-Ashburton Treaty | Atlantic Ocean | Flag | Down East | Timber |
| William King | Landlocked Salmon | Lobster(s) | Counties | Eastern New England Uplands |
| Penobscot | Castine | | American Revolution | Treaty of Paris |
| Sir Ferdinando Gorges | River(s) | Henry Wadsworth Longfellow | Missouri Compromise | Industries |
| Aroostook Plateau | Moose | Lewiston | Massachusetts Bay | Bangor |

# Maine Bingo

| Dominion of New England | Penobscot | Landlocked Salmon | Flag | Bangor |
|---|---|---|---|---|
| Blueberry (-ies) | French Canadians | Legislative Branch | Henry Wadsworth Longfellow | Motto |
| Augusta | Executive Branch | | King Philip | Acadia |
| Nicknames | Wabanaki Confederacy | Portland | Missouri Compromise | River(s) |
| State | Massachusetts Bay | Moose | Timber | Industries |

Maine Bingo: Card No. 20

# Maine Bingo

| William King | Atlantic Ocean | Legislative Branch | Flag | Nicknames |
|---|---|---|---|---|
| Augusta | Industries | Bar Harbor | Down East | Moosehead |
| Canada | Lewiston |  | Penobscot | New England |
| Henry Wadsworth Longfellow | Counties | River(s) | White Pine | Massachusetts Bay |
| King Philip | Moose | Bangor | Border(s) | Missouri Compromise |

# Maine Bingo

| Crop | Sir Ferdinando Gorges | Industries | Aroostook Plateau | Coat of Arms |
|---|---|---|---|---|
| Motto | Landlocked Salmon | Treaty of Paris | Down East | American Revolution |
| Blueberry (-ies) | Eastern New England Uplands | | Moosehead | Executive Branch |
| River(s) | White Pine | Missouri Compromise | Acadia | Legislative Branch |
| Moose | Border(s) | Penobscot | Canada | King Philip |

Maine Bingo: Card No. 22

# Maine Bingo

| Bar Harbor | Penobscot | Counties | Aroostook Plateau | Bangor |
|---|---|---|---|---|
| Atlantic Ocean | Dominion of New England | Lewiston | William King | Acadia |
| Sir Ferdinando Gorges | Coat of Arms | | Portland | Moosehead |
| Canada | Moose | River(s) | Border(s) | Missouri Compromise |
| Nicknames | Wabanaki Confederacy | Massachusetts Bay | Henry Wadsworth Longfellow | Industries |

# Maine Bingo

| | | | | |
|---|---|---|---|---|
| Bar Harbor | Massachusetts Bay | Dominion of New England | Penobscot | Down East |
| Industries | Bangor | Legislative Branch | Motto | Moosehead |
| Executive Branch | Crop | | Coat of Arms | Canada |
| Nicknames | Portland | River(s) | Border(s) | Augusta |
| State | King Philip | Moose | Landlocked Salmon | Wabanaki Confederacy |

# Maine Bingo

| King Philip | Legislative Branch | Penobscot | New England | Industries |
|---|---|---|---|---|
| Acadia | Augusta | William King | Bar Harbor | American Revolution |
| White Pine | Down East | | Portland | River(s) |
| Treaty of Paris | Nicknames | Wabanaki Confederacy | Moose | Eastern New England Uplands |
| Bangor | Dominion of New England | Blueberry (-ies) | Coastal Lowlands | State |

# Maine Bingo

| Industries | Penobscot | Sir Ferdinando Gorges | Motto | Crop |
|---|---|---|---|---|
| Henry Wadsworth Longfellow | Landlocked Salmon | Down East | Dominion of New England | Bar Harbor |
| White Pine | Portland | | Eastern New England Uplands | King Philip |
| Border(s) | Aroostook Plateau | Nicknames | Moose | River(s) |
| Executive Branch | Coastal Lowlands | New England | Wabanaki Confederacy | State |

Maine Bingo: Card No. 26

# Maine Bingo

| | | | | |
|---|---|---|---|---|
| Sir Ferdinando Gorges | Blueberry (-ies) | Penobscot | Dominion of New England | French Canadians |
| Nicknames | Portland | William King | River(s) | American Revolution |
| White Mountains | Wabanaki Confederacy | | Moose | King Philip |
| Crop | Atlantic Ocean | Legislative Branch | State | Acadia |
| Coastal Lowlands | Eastern New England Uplands | Industries | Treaty of Paris | Executive Branch |

# Maine Bingo

| Sir Ferdinando Gorges | Dominion of New England | Treaty of Paris | Penobscot | Bar Harbor |
|---|---|---|---|---|
| French Canadians | Industries | Portland | Motto | Eastern New England Uplands |
| Wabanaki Confederacy | Canada |  | Executive Branch | Henry Wadsworth Longfellow |
| Timber | Crop | Lewiston | Moose | River(s) |
| Aroostook Plateau | Estêvão Gomes | Coastal Lowlands | State | Nicknames |

# Maine Bingo

| Industries | Dominion of New England | Crop | William King | Estêvão Gomes |
|---|---|---|---|---|
| Missouri Compromise | Henry Wadsworth Longfellow | Legislative Branch | Executive Branch | Treaty of Paris |
| White Pine | Portland | | American Revolution | Penobscot |
| French Canadians | Nicknames | Judicial Branch | Moose | River(s) |
| Bar Harbor | Down East | State | Atlantic Ocean | Wabanaki Confederacy |

# Maine Bingo

| Castine | Penobscot | Motto | Estêvão Gomes | River(s) |
|---|---|---|---|---|
| Acadia | Dominion of New England | Sir Ferdinando Gorges | Eastern New England Uplands | American Revolution |
| White Pine | Coat of Arms |  | Executive Branch | Legislative Branch |
| State | Atlantic Ocean | Aroostook Plateau | Moose | Portland |
| Nicknames | Webster-Ashburton Treaty | Wabanaki Confederacy | Industries | Treaty of Paris |

Maine Bingo: Card No. 30

www.ingramcontent.com/pod-product-compliance
Lightning Source LLC
LaVergne TN
LVHW061341060426
835511LV00014B/2052